POIGN

ECHOES
FROM THE DEPTHS OF MY SOUL

Robbie George

ISBN: 0-7596-9650-0 (e-book)
ISBN: 0-7596-9651-9 (Paperback)

This book is printed on acid free paper.

1stBooks – rev. 07/18/03

Dedicated To The Memory Of My Parents:

The Late Reverend & Mrs. R. C. George, Sr.

CONTENTS

The View Beside You

Abiding Love

A Variant Collection

Wrapped In Innocence

A Variant Collection Part II

'Tis Reality

THE VIEW
BESIDE YOU

ଔ

No more, no more

We turn our heads,
When she is abused, molested,
Infused with a strange seed,
Unaware of the tragedy of the dire
deed.

We turn our heads,
When we see a confused, wanton
child,
Carrying a struggling life,
Ignorant of the essence of becoming.

We turn our heads,
While that life develops inside her,
And bursts forth from this child's
womb,
Needy, demanding, labeled,
unwanted.

We turn our heads,
When this wretchedly fettered life
Comes charging at the world,
A tender miracle, yet damned.

We turn our heads,
Knowing this child-mother, herself,
Is inadequate, angry, confused,
Demanding your servitude and
mine.

We turn our heads,
Knowing this new life
Has no father to shoulder the task,
To nurture, teach, discipline, and
love.

We turn our heads
When this oppressive burden
Is passed to society,
Hoping the problem will disappear.

We turn our heads,
When this male child
Is molested, abused, misused,
confused;
But no more, no more.

In silent indignation,
We turn our heads,
Annoyed by this plighted man-
child,
But no more, no more.

This deprived life
Just took another life,
Your mother's, your father's, your
child's,
Yours, mine, his own.

WE SEE NOT WHY

We turn away,
When the task becomes difficult,
While forging uncharted seas,
When nurturing becomes a heavy burden.

We turn away,
When our charge demands our attention;
We see not the turmoil raging inside;
But neglect, like slow poison, destroys.

We turn away,
When tough love becomes unpopular,
Knowing danger, like a fatal summons,
Lurks without, within.

We turn away,
Willing to take ominous risks,
Hoping troublesome problems will
disappear;
Never disciplined, never loved, schooled
on hate.

We turn away,
Indifferent to fundamental need,
Granting peer pressure
Astounding, controlling power.

When we turn away,
Apathy becomes a deadly force,
Like an unpredictable failure,
Poised to maim, destroy.

Like fiery magma below,
Spirits of nature,
Hormones rising, exploding;
No effectual control do they know.

Blood, guts, and tears,
Followed by dashed hopes and hot fears;
Listen to the children's anguish and cry;
Choose love to discover why.

Misinformed, abused, confused,
Your child just took another life;
Your child just lost his dream,
Forever and ever and ever.

I WEEP

I weep for the children,
When their innocence is gone;
I weep for the children
Who long for love,
Whose bodies crave for nurture.

I weep for the children,
Who ache for comfort,
The children who yearn to belong,
Whose hearts
Have been torn asunder.

I weep for the children,
Whose spirits are anemic,
The children who
Crave for understanding,
Whose minds have been warped, polluted.

I weep for the children,
When their world
Is sordid, decadent, lonely,
The children whose souls are deformed,
Whose future is dark, bleak.

I weep for you and me,
Whose solutions
Are complacency, indifference,
Whose hearts are cold, callous,

Whose spirits are diminished, broken.

I weep for you and me,
Who have made our children
The lost children.
I weep for you and me whose fears are real,
Whose world is a future condemned.

I weep, I weep; no more tears,
Just a somber emptiness;
I weep, an aching pain
In my heart and soul;
I weep, I weep, I weep.

Robbie George

I WEEP AND WEEP

I weep for the children,
Who will never know their purpose,
Whose tomorrow
Was decreed hopeless.

I weep for the children
Who will never share
Their hopes and dreams,
Who will never know joy.

I weep for the children,
Who inherited the poison,
That courses through
Their parents' hearts.

I weep for the children,
Whose bodies are
Subservient to deadly forces,
Whose veins are pathways of destruction.

I weep for the children,
Whose minds are befuddled, muddled,
Whose dreams
Are dark, savage.

I weep for the children,
Who will never
Share their gifts, their love;
Whose stay is but a flicker of time.

I weep for the young souls gone astray;
I weep for the souls,
Who will never
Find their way.

I weep for the souls
Of the uncommitted,
Trapped by powers whose reins are tight,
Whose harvest is perversely ripe.

I weep for the innocent, the pure,
Befell by unseen calamities,
Who knew not
What divine wisdom proclaims.

INNOCENCE

I saw a child of ten,
Rocking her baby to sleep last night.
I heard her tender voice
As she sang a lullaby:
"Now go to sleep, baby doll,
And don't you cry,
I'll learn to be a mother by-and-by."

I saw a child of thirteen,
Rocking her baby to sleep one day.
I heard her tender voice
As she sang a lullaby:
"Close your eyes, little one
And don't you cry,
Your daddy will love me by-and-by."

I watched a child of fifteen,
Rocking her baby to sleep today.
I heard her tender voice
As she sang a lullaby:
"Now hush, big man, don't you cry,
I know your daddy didn't plan to die."

Alone in a tortuous maze,
Heart and soul not in control,
Tender bodies distorted,
Unknown innocence aborted,
Life's dreams
Forever thwarted.

Needy baby
Has learned a new song;
Needy baby
Sits rocking and singing all day long,
A low mournful sound,
Echoing her pain and emptiness.

Needy baby sits
Rocking and singing all day long;
Needy baby has learned a song of misery;
Needy baby
Sits staring into space,
Encumbered by her own worldly grace.

You children who children produce,
What curse
Has befallen thee;
You have bodies ready to bear,
While your heart
Lacks the wisdom to care.

A FRAGILE FLOWER

You sow wild oats among the weeds so wild;
"It's the natural thing to do," you say;
The deeds of some become others' sorrow;
Life's never naught nor so raisonne.

I am one begot,
Among the weeds so wild;
I am but a fragile flower;
I am an innocent child.

I am that I am;
I became as you ordained,
Conceived by the wiles of man.
How false your virtue you maintained.

I am a rare flower,
Growing on the rocky hillside;
I have known hard times;
My life's like an ebbing tide.

I have been misused,
And often abused;
Still, I am a rare flower,
As rare as a whispering star;
I inspire your heart with my touch.

The tale I weave
Is not intended to please;
When the children cry
Tears of anguish and pain,
Then you only sigh.

Reality fosters the truth;
When the children die,
A travesty to behold,
How dare you cry.

Have mercy on the children,
Sown among the weeds so wild;
I see no face,
Just a form without meaning,
Only a soul labeled chaste.

Robbie George

How do i become a man

I must learn how to become a man.
The road is sorely rough and rocky;
I dare not embrace the ultimate mistake;
I ponder which path I must take.

Please show me the way;
The maze deepens day by day;
Hormones raging inside,
Charging like waves at high tide.

Many contradictions abound;
The elusive answers I've never found.
Heart and soul not in control;
I know not what virtue morals extol.

Uncertainty looms everywhere;
Never knew a manly hand;
I stand alone like grains of sand;
Won't you show me how to be a man.

RESPONSIBILITY

Hunger pains
Gnawed at his innards;
His last meal was yesterday;
Just a piece of bread would do,
A cup of milk too.

He snuggled close
To the warmth of his two
companions;
His body heat they too, would
share;
The night would be long, cold, and
lonely;
Only one light burned overhead.

Upon the dawn's awakening,
He readied himself
For his big challenge;
He made his way
To the corner neighborhood store.

He drew attention
As soon as he ventured
Through the door;
Heavy, clouded eyes
Sought his every move;
A piece of bread, a cup of milk.

He headed out the door,
Precious possessions in tow;
Heavy hands
Upon his person descended,
Giant hands, giant demeanor;
Loud voices, an inimical cacophony.

Into a cold, metal conveyer
He was tossed;
Fear and dread descended,
Like a foggy nightmare;
He directed all to his place
Called home.

Heavy hands banged the door;
Doom expected for evermore;
Heavy shoes hit the floor,
Crunching glass and needles
As they bore.

The giants adjusted,
To the dim of sight,
As two whimpering young siblings,
With sad, sallow eyes met their
stare,
Alarmed to see them standing there.

Cold, hungry, in piteous disarray,
Too young to know,
Their six-year-old brother
Had just risked his life,
For a piece of bread, a cup of milk.

REMEMBER ME

Remember me when I'm gone,
My stay here won't be very long;
I walk the dark streets of time;
The paths I take all seem wrong.

I don't know who I am;
I know not the way to your heart;
Out of touch, out of mind,
This burden is tearing me apart.

Like the thirsty river, never quenching,
I prowl the streets day and night,
Looking for that elusive dream;
I have never known wrong from right.

I have known sorrow and heartache,
I writhe with heavy, hot pain;
I ache for the spirit missing from my
 soul;
Life's essence I can not explain.

I know life's tumultuous way;
I wander in a tangled maze,
Roaming the back roads and alleys,
Stumbling, blundering, as in a daze.

By day, I wear a lonely heart,
And long for the night to begin;
I'm next to you, but not of you;
In darkness, I become the hunter again.

I walk the highway of dark, hard stone;
I was born in sin and inequity;
Existence is sorely bewildering;
Won't you stop and rescue me.

THE SUMMON

Kevin woke up in a deep cold sweat;
Just like the nights before,
The nightmares had returned,
Foretelling of heartache and woe.

Hot metal missiles,
Splintering bone,
Spattering brains, guts, and pain,
Shattering unanchored hopes, dreams.

Hot metal missiles,
Red hot blood on cold concrete,
A pulsating life instantly exterminated;
Dreams dissolved in the wind.

Hot metal missiles,
Essence of being snatched away,
Condemning to hell's eternity;
Memories lingering only in decay.

Hot metal missiles,
Mama, grandma, six younger siblings,
Bent grievously in stormy sorrow;
Hopes dismal for another tomorrow.

Hot metal missiles,
Calamitous, deadly, lethal, fatal;
He was just a misfit; never knew his place;
Fourteen years too short,
Never realized who he was.

LISTEN

Listen to the little children,
They have a story to tell;
They are the witnesses to salvation.

Listen to the little children,
They are the innocent of you and me;
They are pure love and loyalty.

Listen to the little children,
Feel their suffering and pain;
Their tears and agony your soul stain.

Why suffer the little children?
None has fathomed nor framed,
The depth of sacrifice proclaimed.

Listen to the little children,
They will teach you how to suffer;
They will teach you how to be strong.

Listen to the little children,
Hear their lost dreams;
Grow strong in their sacrifice.

Listen to the little children;
They will teach you how to live;
They will teach you how to die.

Listen to the songs of the little children,
Listen to the joy of the little children;
They are God's soldiers of the cross.

Listen to the little children,
For you and me they cry,
For humanity they die.

Robbie George

I AM UNIQUE

It took a long time
For me to realize
That there is no one like me;
I am who I am; fate did decree.

I feel good about myself;
I am me and nobody else.
I can walk and I can talk;
I can think; I am unique.

As I look in a mirror,
I see just an image staring there;
But it's deep inside
That the true me abides.

My feelings and thoughts
Are there,
My heart and soul applaud
What makes me who I am.

I feel good about myself;
I am me and nobody else.
I can walk and I can talk;
I can think; I am unique.

I ask you to be my guide;
Walk by my side; show me love;
Show that you care.
It's so simple; love can be everywhere.

I feel good about myself;
I am me and nobody else.
I can walk and I can talk;
I can think; I am unique.

Just open your heart and feel the power
That comes,
From loving someone like me;
I will grow and love you in return.

I feel good about myself;
I am me and nobody else.
I can walk and I can talk.
I can think; I am unique.

Robbie George

THE HEART OF A CHILD

I didn't know I was poor.
The sun-bleached shutters
Against the peeling paint,
The rain-soaked gutters,
The muddy puddles,
These all seemed the scheme of things.

The coffee aroma,
Blending with scrambled eggs,
Streak-a-lean sizzling in the pan,
Biscuits a mountain tall,
With home-made jam, butter and all,
I didn't know I was poor.

Pickled beets and pigs' feet,
My favorite,
Turned-slow Sunday ice cream,
Speckled pinto beans
And shimmering summer greens,
I didn't know I was poor.

Big brother's hand-me-downs,
Warm cotton bee-vee-dees,
Intended to discourage
An unwanted sneeze;
I didn't know I was poor.

The spring rabbit chase,
The three-legged race,
Flaunting yellow daffodils,
Swaying high on a windy hill,
I didn't know I was poor.

The tall willowy carrots,
The hot radishes red,
My pullet that took all day
Her maiden egg to lay;
I didn't know I was poor.

The walk to church,
Through golden leaves of fir,
The picnic spread,
After the benediction was said,
I didn't know I was poor.

A really sound spanking,
With mom complaining:
"It hurts me more than you;
It's wise not to do some things you do;"
I didn't know I was poor.

A good-night kiss,
After a much needed scrubbing,
A prayer at night,
Shutting out the dark with light;
I didn't know I was poor.

Piggy-back rides on dad's tired back,
Mom's scary tales about swamp rattlers,
And things that go thump in the night,
Sure to cause a dreadfully tingling fright;
I didn't know I was poor.

A walk by the graveyard
On a black, moonless night,
Errant winds,
Moaning through nearby trees,
Causing one's hair to slowly bristle,
While silencing dad's valiant whistle;
I didn't know I was poor.

Snow flakes,
Caught on an outstretched tongue,
Mud-crawling in a crawfish pond,
Leaping gushing water holes,
While setting myriads of unknown goals;
I didn't know I was poor.

Mom admonishing,
"Sit up straight, never slouch;
Hold your head up high, never doubt;
Respect yourself and others too;
Good character can elevate you;"
I didn't know I was poor.

Dad advising,
"Never pretend fidelity;
With freedom comes responsibility;
Work is a friend of necessity;
Never trifling you should be."
I didn't know I was poor.

A stolen glance
At a hopeful romance,
Whenever I got the chance;
Mom and dad told me I was loved;
Nobody told me I was poor.

BIG BOY

I want to be like you, big boy;
I want to talk like you;
I want to laugh like you.

I want to walk like you;
Let me hold your hand.
Please teach me how to be a man.

Can I run like the wind?
Will I grow tall like an oak tree?
I'll try, just you wait and see.

Will I grow strong just like you?
Will you forever stay with me?
Will I die with you by my side?

When will I leave this bed?
So small is this space;
Will I ever wander to another place?

Will I ever walk barefoot on the grass so green?
The flowers are swaying in the breeze;
Why can't I sway; why can't I run?

I want to chase the butterflies,
Feel the wind in my face;
Let me be like boys and girls out yonder.

I have never known hate;
I have known the love,
Of Him who comforts me.

What will you teach me?
I can teach you how to suffer;
Won't you teach me how to live?

TOMORROW BECOMES TODAY

I've been here before,
But, Oh! so long ago:
The waning, midnight moon,
The shadows on the lake,
The dew-soaked grass at daybreak.

Watching and waiting,
Holding firmly to my matchless gift,
Lest the wolves of the night,
Like mangled, tangled dreams,
Attack and devour.

Heart filled with despair;
I see anger on young boys' faces;
I see malice in young children's eyes;
I sense hatred in your heart;
Today is a sad remembrance.

A six-foot thirteen-year-old man-child
Cried, when ordered to tell the time of day,
A pang to the very soul;
The children snickered;
I cried.

His blood runs warm;
He sleeps; He hungers;
He laughs, occasionally;
Pinch him, cut him, he bleeds;
Crush him, he cries; kill him, he too dies.

Though we look intensely
In the looking glass,
We see not ourselves
As others do;
Arrogance, like a mourning veil, Blinds.

LITTLE ONES

Why don't you believe in Me,
Little ones, little ones?
Why don't you believe in Me?
Monsters are only in your mind;
Monsters are only in your mind.

Believe in Me, believe in Me;
Then, you will surely find,
That I am loving,
Protective and kind;
Believe in Me, believe in Me.

What are you dreaming little ones?
Are you truly troubled, little ones?
Is your world so bleak, little ones?
Is your life so dreary?
Or, is it only in your mind?

Why are you sad and melancholy?
Is the world so cruel, little ones?
Are people so angry and mean?
Do they destroy your dreams?
Or, is it only in your mind?

Nobody loves you little ones?
Nobody cares?
Believe in Me, little ones;
Believe in Me and you will find,
Monsters are only in your mind.

ALL I WANT

All I want forever is a family,
Someone to love me, someone to care,
Someone loving and kind,
Someone to trust me, someone to share.

All I want forever is a family;
I'll take a sister, a little girl, like me,
One who can walk and talk,
Just a little girl I can touch and see.

All I want is one little girl,
A girl who can laugh and cry,
Someone who can play house,
One whose world I can help beautify.

I'll take a little brother too,
If one can be found,
One not too bossy or rough,
One who would not kick me around.

I know I can't climb a tree or hit a ball,
But I'll learn if they want to teach me;
I would, I really would,
Just you wait and see.

But most of all,
The most important thing, yet,
I want a mommy and daddy too,
Now that, I can never forget.

I would be so good;
I'd clean my room through and through,
Even the whole house,
If they wanted me to.

I won't ask for much,
Only a toy or three, a dress of blue,
A doggie, a cat, a parrot,
Or just one or two pets will do.

All I want forever is a family:
A mommy, a daddy, a little sister, too,
And a loving brother,
Who would be kind and true.

I'm going to get me a family:
"Say Mister, I'm not pretty or a celebrity;
I'm just a little girl;
Would you like to be a dad to me?

I know I'm not very tall,
But I can grow to be;
I'm loving and kind;
So don't you want a little girl like me?"

"Miss, if you have a little girl and boy,
Then, you would agree,
They could be a loving
Sister and brother to me."

Robbie George

Honestly, all I want is a family;
Please, loving family, be my family too;
Love and cherish me,
Just as I would love and cherish you.

ABIDING LOVE

ભ

FACELESS

She stood at the 19th.
And "U" Street bus stop.
Face barren of expression,
Eyes cast straight ahead,
Tired, swollen, red.

Her thoughts
Were a distance removed;
Like an antediluvian relic
She was alone
In the crowd.

Her square jaws were set
With a fierce determination;
They belied
The anguish her soul
Had endured.

She had tramped
The five blocks to the bus stop;
Undaunted by the freezing rain,
She stood still;
Like a motion suspended in time,
She waited.

Tonight was no different;
She would board
The lumbering machine
And reach her destination,
Without flaw.

Her black and white oxfords,
Slightly reeling and dented,
Told of having belonged
To another,
Before her.

Her long, army-gray wool coat,
Curled about her swollen ankles,
Intended to provide comfort
From the cold,
Was soaked.

Her face showed of forty years
Of wear;
Her haunched shoulders,
Carried many more
Of despair.

Her chaffed, used hands,
Told of toil, lack of care;
Her hair showed strands of gray,
Her demeanor,
Of decay.

She clutched
A greased, brown paper bag,
Full of unwanted portions
From another's meal.

It was half past seven;
She had stayed
To serve the dinner,
She had prepared earlier.

The day's unremitting toil
Had left her weary and exhausted,
Her body numb,
Heart and soul disquieted.

The bus arrived,
And like a creature
Fashioned from man's hands,
She moved with the crowd.

Benumbed, like a fresh corpse,
She would rest her tired body
During the ride,
Respite for a fleeting moment.

But her mind kept remembering;
Her burdened heart kept aching;
She had buried her husband
Just five years past.

She was eminently aware,
Her next job
Always awaited,
At the end of her journey.

As she turned her key in the lock
And opened the door,
Five eager, young faces
Greeted her with glee.

Though the day
Had grown used and old,
Mom was finally home;
All was well with their world.

UNCERTAINTIES

It was early March, 1964.
She boarded
The 6:05 A.M. "Federal Triangle"
At East Capitol and Benning Road, S.E.

The walk to the bus stop
Had been most exhilarating;
To her,
All was well.

The sky had been painted
A brilliant azure;
The birds' harmonies
Still echoed in her head;
The morning air was nippy and crisp.

The stalwart, early-morning souls
About her,
Seemed pleasant and happy,
As they, like her,
Hurried and scurried about.

Her small, contented world,
At that moment in time,
Seemed balanced
And peaceful.

The four-block walk to the bus stop,
Had caused the developing child
Within her,
To wage his usual protest:
Thumping and kicking.

This was expected and welcomed.
As she struggled aboard
The standing-room-only bus,
The movements
Became more pronounced.

She was not alarmed;
This had happened many times before;
She was into her eighth month
Of pregnancy.

Among the multitude
Of standing passengers,
She found a position
And held onto a vertical rod,
As she attempted to brace herself.

Just then,
The jerking vehicle
Moved out into the steady stream
Of early morning traffic.

As the lumbering conveyer
Moved along its route,
Her mountainous, jerking body,
Moved in painful rhythm.

45

Intermittent stops
Were multitudinous, rough;
So the agonizing experience
Was continually increased..

As the bus wound
Along its meandering route,
Picking up more fares,
The standing-room-only
Became very pregnant, like her.

No man,
No woman,
No child,
Offered her a seat.

When she finally arrived
At 12th. and Constitution, NW,
And attempted to depart from the bus,
She could barely move,
As her body ached with intense pain.

Her unborn child
Had been jarred, jolted and jounced;
As his world was threatened and assaulted,
This child, in his agony,
Was struggling and protesting.

As she slowly moved her body,
Writhing in pain,
Along the three long blocks to her office,
She prayed;
And as she prayed, she was given a revelation.

She did not know the meaning of the vision;
She just knew that her unborn child's world
Had been assaulted,
And pain was racking their bodies and her soul.

Upon arriving at her office,
She sat down and began to write.
The message she wrote is called,
"Reckoning."

RECKONING

Now is the time for man
To examine
The very essence of his being.
When man's gods become allies
In his insane acts against his fellow man,
It is time for reckoning.

When the Word of God,
Becomes but an illusion
In man's heart and soul,
When mortals rage and thirst
For the blood of their brothers,
It is time for reckoning.

When jealousy and hate become diseases,
Tempered by woeful ignorance,
When insatiable greed,
Becomes the catalytic force
In man's deeds,
It is time for reckoning.

When indifference is adopted,
As the supreme mode of behavior,
When that minute strand of morality,
Forsakes man in that moment
Of dire peril,
It is time for reckoning.

When vanity and arrogance entwine,
And cleave with a tenacity
Like the ancient gnarled pine,
When the mind loses its focus,
And the heart becomes set like stone,
It is time for reckoning.

When love and devotion,
Become but obsolete debris,
When the heart becomes callous,
And the soul rent by dismay,
It is time for reckoning.

When wisdom becomes
An adversary of truth,
When blood runs deep on numerous
shores,
And a troubled and uncertain world
Teeters on the abyss of destruction,
It is time for reckoning.

A VARIANT
COLLECTION

༺༻

Silence

The deadly silence
Swept over the room,
Impaling the combatants,
Like the fingers of death
In a chilly tomb.

No sound was made;
One dared not move,
Lest he too encountered
The presence of doom.

Unspeakable was the cause;
Unpardonable the sin;
No one wonders why,
Others did not win.

Robbie George

HERE AND THEN

He sits alone, pondering his past,
Never mindful of today;
He sits alone, waiting for that visitor,
Who was late yesterday.

He sits alone,
Content to let the world go by;
A cauldron of adolescent fears,
Rivers of briny tears.

I HOWL

I howl like an animal,
In the night;
My heart is so in distress,
My iniquity stands bold,
No peace for my tortured soul;
Untold victims I have claimed,
I howl and howl;
No rest, no tranquility,
Enemy at my door,
Nightmares tell of sins of yore,
I howl and howl;
My soul stained with unsightly blood,
No cleansing, no peace, no rest;
I howl like the wolf in the night,
Blood-thirsty, needy, obsessed;
I know not what color purity,
Shades and shades in between,
I long for you to make me clean;
From the darkest pit,
I have ascended;
Layers and layers of darkness abound;
I keep searching and searching
For higher ground,
Less fraught with woes and agony,
Less darker than the one I have found.
My tainted past
Can't be made pure again;
When degradation is your keep,

Robbie George

You can never return to chastity.
A ray of sunshine
Challenges your sanity.
When purity is debased,
We accept what takes its place.
The stains I can not remove,
The anguish is forever etched in my soul,
My sins, my heart can nev'r disprove.
By vanity one falls from grace,
Then evil, takes its place,
And your soul it does deface.

BROTHER PIETY

As I passed your way,
I tried to reach you,
But, I did not stoop low enough.

If, with just a simple gesture,
I can alter your falling grace,
This, I will do.

But, do not expect me to crawl,
Just to save one,
So low as you.

Robbie George

HONOR

When man in his ascent,
Loses the common touch,
His fall is inevitable.

Between the fine line
Of here and there,
Lies a plane of noble compromise.

THE OLD YOUNG MEN

They are the old young men,
With stooped shoulders,
Jerky hand,
And shaky dispositions.

They are the old young men,
Ancient,
As the sands of time,
Endowed with the choice sublime.

They are the old young men,
Scorned by the evil
In their hearts;
Debauch, debase, deadly, deceitful.

They are the heritage
Of the yesteryears,
Creators of the image today,
Destroyers of the ideal tomorrow.

They are impotent, calculating men;
Unwise.
They are the essence of all that was,
All that is , and all that is to be.

They are personified
By what was in the beginning,
Sowers of the seeds that pervade
The hell of tears, grief, damnation.

They are the button pushers,
The deal makers,
The morals breakers.
They are the perverts of ideal
purity.

They are the walking dead,
Heart and soul in hock,
Brain addled,
In the head.

They are the essence of the evil
That has been,
That is,
And all that is to be.

MYSTERIES

Spring comes on an unseen breeze,
And its stay is but a short while,
Winter's way just to appease.

The memorable moments, days,
So precious, so tender, so few,
Life's message blooms anew.

I awakened,
And was tenderly kissed
By the warmth of the morning's sun.

As I wandered there and yonder,
The sun shone with all its brilliance,
Blinding, confusing.

Like a foreboding mystery,
The beginning of an ending
Descended upon me.

Shaking, I wondered what strangeness
Had my soul so engulfed,
Or had I so blithely embraced.

The race, the face were of me.
My mind was questioning
This newly arrived decree.

Robbie George

Buds that appeared in late spring-time,
Became fully opened blossoms,
Drooping in the summer's hot heat.

I was exposed,
In the innocence of my youth,
Not choked, but bombarded
By the essence of reality.

Being is strange,
Hurting,
Savage;
But life is wonderful.

JOHN CALVERT ROACH

Perched on the shelf
For the world to see,
Was none other than thee,
Arrogant John Calvert Roach.

You came right in
As invited guest;
But really John,
You are an unwanted pest.

Free lodgings you demand
And boldly you encroach,
But comeuppance is surely due,
Mr. John Calvert Roach.

So mind not if upon your frame I step;
Though the squish-squash I detest,
I loathe you more you pest.

Robbie George

THE GIFT

So tender, so innocent, so new,
Wondrous, blessed gift,
So much a part of you.

Love, protect, and hold,
Keep close to your racing heart;
Myriads of mysteries yet to unfold.

Sundry hills will erode away,
Venturing beyond the bounds of time;
Only the essence of the moment

Is willed to stay.

WILDFLOWER

Wildflower, wildflower,
Sprite of sun, wind, and rain;
Thou beauty and mystery
Only God doth ordain.

Wildflower, wildflower,
Free as a breeze,
Myriads of haughty choices,
Apt to wander where you please.

LOVE AND DIGNITY

The tattered old crone
Sat in the gutter,
Leafing through the pages
Of yesterday.

A reject of society,
A forgotten relic of the past,
A grievous eyesore,
A blemish so demeaning.

She is but a forgotten mother;
She rocked the cradle at night,
And caressed the needy,
To make things right.

She is forgotten;
How short the memory,
How cold grows the heart,
How mindlessly we all play part.

She is weary,
But rest is denied her tired body;
She is lonely,
But companions, she has none.

She is sick,
But there is no comforting hand;
She is destitute, desolate;
Tomorrow, she dies in a foreign
land.

NEVER DAUNTED

She runs the gauntlet,
Blocking adversity
Along the way,
Smoothing the rough roads,
Guarding against harm and dismay.

With a tender touch, a loving smile,
She eases the pain, lightens the load,
Loving and assuring
All the while;
She is woman.

She is strength, inspiration, joy;
She is calm in the storm;
She is the sunshine
That keeps you warm;
She is woman.

She walks in a dignity all her own;
She is wife, sister, mother;
Just and virtuous deeds
She has shown;
She is woman.

She is a little lower
Than the angels;
She is the Christ Child's Mother;
She is glorified, sanctified;
She is woman.

Guard her well,
As she dims in the night;
Treat her gently as she loses her light;
Rest her weary head upon your arm;
Cradle her closely to keep her warm.

Days and nights have come and gone;
She takes her place in the setting sun,
Leaving the race for you and me to run;
She is woman.

Ease her down gently,
Where the sycamore grows,
Where the warbler croons
'Til late eventide,
And where peace and tranquility abide;
She is woman.

Reveries

As you haunt my late-night dreams,
And transform my morning reveries,
I endure the pain my heart unforesees.

I seek your touch, your tender kiss,
But this can never be,
Your love remains forever elusory.

I watched you walk a lonely road,
And remember that though apart,
You possess my soul and heart.

Years have come and gone;
My love you will never know,
In my dreams it will only show.

A FOOL'S FOOLISH FOLLY

I to a fool's folly have trod;
Too often spoken words
Land on critical ears,

Rapidly to be torn, criticized,
And stamped
A fool's foolish folly.

MOMENTS

Capture each rapturous moment,
Fasten it to your heart and soul;
Its existence is sorely temporal,
And the very essence of life
Is ephemeral.

Capture the moment;
Hear the crooning nightingale,
Flitting near the weeping springs,
Hypnotizing all by the melodies
He sings.

Capture the moment;
Smell the fragrance
Of the honeysuckle,
Drifting on whimsical breezes,
Free to wander wherever it pleases.

Capture the moment;
Behold
The glow of flickering lights,
Dancing on a distant shore,
Sharing memories to last for evermore.

Capture the moment;
To this lofty height she bore me,
Here to linger momentarily;
Other worlds
Are yet to be known.

Time, like some mysterious vapor,
Moves on, and on, and on.
The change, unseen, unknowingly,
Creeps in,
And shouts life's brevity.

THE HEARTBEAT

What makes the heart hold
To its diverse inclination,
Remains a mystery
To unfold.

I wear the cloak of despair;
Beneath strains every fiber to impart
The quintessence
Of a plighted heart.

Thou in a wondrous melody awakens
The fiery essence of my spirit,
And in thy majestic beauty,
The truth is implicit.

Let me run;
Let me fly;
Let me feel the stormy blast;
Let me live, love, cry.

Let me gaze at the rippling brook,
Wander through the covers
Of a well-loved book;
Oh! let me dream, dream, dream.

Let me dream
Of elves, castles and fairytales;
Let me dream of worlds unknown,
And whispered promises yet unsown.

Let me dream
Of stories not yet born;
Let me feel the wind in my hair today;
Let it take my ebbing breath away.

Let me know
Of Beings supreme;
Let me stretch tall while I climb;
Today I claim as sublime.

Let me walk; let me saunter
Through the tall, dew-soaked clover;
Let me dance in the meadow,
As I cross over.

JOURNEYS

Fate bestows damnation upon the innocent;
With a body ravished by disease and decay,
I need time to rest and mend,
Much time you need to lend.

But there is never enough to hold,
I have journeys to make untold.
Hell's naught but what's within;
The will is mine to break or bend.

The cosmic lot which befalls us all,
Is willed by the foe of yore,
And we, the creatures of the day,
Rule to conquer and suffer to stay.

STRANGER

I sit among you, but I am alone;
I sit among you, I am my own,
A proud, independent spirit.
I see you now, then you are gone.

I sit among you,
We are strangers in a common place,
Strangers for a common deed,
Strangers filling a common need.

I sit among you;
You deem me the hunter,
Then you become the prey;
For tomorrow comes only in your mind.

I walk among you;
I don't know your name,
I don't know your joy,
I can't fathom your pain.

Night wanders yonder,
And day creeps hither;
Spring evolves into awareness,
Then summer awakens into full bloom.

With a gentle touch and caress,
The harbinger takes its place,
And coaxes from restful repose,
Infinite wonders unknown.

75

I sit among you;
Strangers we were yesterday;
Friends we must become today;
Eras past have fashioned a common legacy.

You, who believe in your own eminence,
Humility could offer a clue,
That there are others
More gifted than you.

You don't know my name;
You can't fathom my pain;
I've traveled a long, treacherous road;
I've become more tolerant, wiser.

I am not an evil invader;
Goodness shines through my eyes;
Truth is in my step;
All can never be seen nor fathomed.

 I walk among you;
My steps are slower; my eyes are dim.
There is no compassion for me;
I wonder where the shadows have gone.

Time is dying, never to be awakened;
Destiny lies over the horizon;
Together, let us walk,
Toward tomorrow's elusive promise.

THE JOURNEY

Crying, she stood at the foot of my bed,
Suspended over a fiery blast,
And bade me go,
To yonder places I did not know.

Awash by a haunting dread,
Engulfed in pain and sorrow,
A wretched soul was she,
Writhing in agony beyond degree.

As we traveled through eternity,
Speeding through time and space,
I could but sense and tell,
Our journey was taking us straight to hell.

A place of doom and anguish,
Lost souls condemned to agony;
Moldy forms of humanity I did see,
Stretching forever in infinity.

Floating like transformed beings,
Transported on a breath of time,
Onward and onward we traveled,
As dreadful visions unraveled.

Lost souls who willed their fate,
Trapped forever in throes of misery,
Blood dripping from bodies galore,
Suffering and pain for evermore.

Robbie George

The journey foretold tales of woe;
I prayed as we traveled
The whole night long,
And awoke to find my mother gone.

MINERVA

On a misty chilly morn,
As the fog rolled in and out,
I caught a glimpse of her,
As her slate gray head
Bobbed there and about,
Bringing hate, death, and despair.

Then, on a stormy day,
I saw her riding the clouds,
Like a fiery mist;
She came spinning, tumbling,
Falling about in a radiant hue,
On those dark rolling clouds of blue.

Closer and closer she came;
Heavier and heavier my heart pounded;
Onward and onward she came,
Always ready her victims to claim;
And I knew,
What was meant to be for thee.

LOVE UNFULFILLED

Let lie the embers
That smolder in the dark;
Stir not in a draft,
Lest you start a spark.

I dreamt last night of a love unfulfilled,
Stored in the recesses of my heart,
There to linger until,
The dawn encases me in a chill.

And yet the fervent hope lingers still,
That the gods intercede and will,
I upon such a journey embark,
'Til my heart sings like the meadowlark.

While time holds my true love fast,
My sentimental journey can nev'r last.
From my haunting dream I'll arouse,
And let lie the embers that smolder in the dark.

BORN A WOMAN

I was born a woman,
So I know the agony of needing you.
I was born a woman,
So I know the thrill of loving you.

I was born a woman,
So I know the fear of wanting you.
I was born a woman,
And just like a woman, I love you.

I was born a woman;
I want you;
I was born a woman;
I need you.

I was born a woman;
I need you for now and for always;
So I accept
The pain and joy of loving you.

LET ME WALK AWAY

My love for him I can not hide;
I was foolish,
I made a mistake,
But I've got my pride.
Let me be woman enough
To walk away.

I've cried and I've cried,
But I know my tears are in vain;
To forget him,
I have really, really tried;
Please, let me be woman enough
To walk away.

To say he's sorry won't ease the
pain;
He was untrue to another,
And with me,
He will be unfaithful again;
Let me be woman enough
To walk away.

I didn't know how dreadful
The pain would feel;
I've never felt such agony before;
I don't know if the wound will ever
heal;
Just let me be woman enough
To walk away.

Life can be so barren, cold, and
cruel;

But I know,
My heart can't hurt like yesterday,
And I hope somehow the wound
will heal;
But for now, let me be woman
enough
To walk away.

Robbie George

THE MELODY

I can't capture this haunting melody;
It just keeps slipping away.
Somewhere in my head it rings,
But my heart won't let it sing.

I'm so lonely since you've been gone;
I just keep trying to capture the melody,
The one you sang to me,
When we were young and fancy-free.

I walk the streets alone,
I want to feel the magic from your touch,
I need the fire from your kiss,
But, they are forever amiss.

I'm caught in a cloudy heap,
I'm confused, darn nearly abused.
I can't eat; I can't sleep;
It's because of you I bitterly weep.

If I find in my heart that I love you,
If I find that I truly care,
Turn me over easy, pity my agony;
The melody was never meant for me.

VISIONS

You catch my eye
As you go strolling by;
You tease me with your smile,
As your eyes beguile all the while,
You luscious vision of my imagination.

My heart swells
And my pulse rises and tells;
You hypnotize with your walk,
You mesmerize with your talk,
You luscious vision of my imagination.

My composure can not hide
The turmoil you cause inside;
You show no shame,
You simply fan the flame,
You luscious vision of my imagination.

It just can't be love;
I'm too much above
This strange petty emotion;
I accept no such notion,
You naughty vision of my imagination.

But my heart can not explain
This throbbing, sensuous pain;
I don't know if it's day or night,
Something just doesn't seem right,
You luscious vision of my imagination.

I don't know why I seem sizzling hot,
When my head says I'm not;
You confuse my body and mind;
Your tactics are so unkind,
You luscious vision of my imagination.

There is nothing wrong with me,
Just you wait and see;
Your delightful assaults will end,
Then my heart will surely mend;
You are only a vision of my imagination.

LOVE LOST

I've been here before,
But oh, so long ago.
The shadows cast on the lake,
The dew-soaked grass at daybreak.

Watching and waiting,
Heart filled with despair;
You felt my presence,
But knew not my essence.

Time was not ripe;
Wills were strong,
Needs were great,
Obligations grievously heavy.

Commitment seemed so wrong;
But, I should have known,
Your green and sun-shiny days;
Your ardor, I should have touched.

Just like the river's water ran deep
On a hot summer's day,
A breeze cooled your sweltering
brow,
And you slowly slipped away.

Robbie George

WRAPPED
IN INNOCENCE

☙

THANK YOU MOM AND DAD
FOR BABY BROTHER

I have a baby brother;
May I hold him, please?

I have a baby brother;
He's like me, but different.

He has tiny fingers;
He has tiny toes too.

May I count them, Please?
1, 2, 3, 4, 5.

Look, mom, two tiny feet!
Look, mom, two tiny hands!

Dad, is he mine, all mine?
I'll take good care of him.

I'll give him my ball and bat;
I'll ride him on my bike.

I'll teach him how to talk;
I'll teach him how to walk.

I'll feed him, just wait and see,
I'll dry him, just like you did me.

Robbie George

He can sleep in my bed;
My arm can cradle his little head.

Please, may I keep him?
Is he mine, all mine?

Now, little brother, don't you cry,
I'll sing you a lullaby.

I'll take good care of you;
Big brothers know what to do.

I'll learn everything somehow;
I'm your big brother now.

Thank you, dad and mom;
I love my little brother.

I LOVE MY MOM AND DADDY TOO

I love my mom,
But I wish my mom weren't so fat.

Joey's mom rides her bike with him.
She even plays softball with Joey.

My mother has trouble walking,
So I don't ask her to play ball with me.

I wish she would,
But I don't want to worry her.

I came home with a black eye,
The other day.

Timmy had yelled,
"David's mom looks like a big hippo."

I didn't mean to slug him;
He deserved it though.

I help my mom a lot;
I put her shoes on her feet.

Sometimes, I get stuff from upstairs.
Her legs hurt so badly.

Robbie George

Dad yells at mom a lot;
She only cries.

I know mom eats too much;
She eats all the time.

I wish I knew what to do,
To make mom skinny again.

I wonder if she knows how much I hurt;
I feel her pain.

And sometimes, I feel dad's pain too;
It just breaks my heart.

DADDY

Daddy, please come home;
I don't see you much anymore.

My team won seven games
So far this season;

I made a home run the last game,
Just for you.

I wish you could have seen it;
It sailed, and sailed, and sailed.

I wish I could fly like that ball;
Then maybe, I could search for you.

I'm seven now;
I've got my two front teeth back.

The older kids don't laugh,
And call me "snaggle tooth" any more.

I know I'm growing up;
But I don't know what to do,
When mom cries in bed.

I promise to be good,
If you only come home.

Tommy's dad is coaching our team;
Tommy's so proud.

I would be proud of you too, dad,
If you just come home.

P.S.: I love you, dad.

MAMA

Mama, Mama,
I wonder where she has gone;
Mama, Mama, please come home.

Bright lights, bright lights,
The streets have stolen Mama;
No goodnight hugs and kisses.

Mama wore her short red dress
Last night.
She looked so pretty,
With her high-heel shoes,
Fish net stocking,
And dangling earrings.

Her lips were bright red,
Just like her long, long fingernails;
She smelled so good,
Like sweet-smelling honeysuckle.

She promised me sneakers,
If I would be brave
And not afraid of the dark.
But I do get afraid and sad,
When Mama goes away.

So I cry and cry;
I dry my tears,
Then I kneel down on my knees

And pray.

Little Tommy woke up;
He cried and cried;
He wanted some milk,
But I had to save it for Cynthia,
So he just cried himself to sleep.

Tommy is only a little kid,
You know.
His fourth birthday
Won't be for seven more months.

Cynthia didn't even wake up
For her twelve o'clock bottle.
I was so glad;
I gave it to her,
When she woke up the next
morning.

Sometimes Mama gets home late.
Last week she was very late;
Some guy beat her up.

She was not so pretty;
Her eyes were black;
One eye was shut.
Her lips were swollen too.

Mama cried and cried;
Tommy and I cried too.
Cynthia screamed.

I gave her a bottle,
But she still screamed.
I took her in my arms,
I rocked back and forth,
Back and forth, back and forth.

Then I gave her the bottle again;
She gulped down all the milk;
She must have been very hungry.

I stayed home
From school that day;
First grade is easy;
I can already read all my letters.

I can count to one hundred;
I know how to read many words;
I can read better
Than all my classmates.

I want to be a doctor, just like Dr.
John.
He gives us our shots;
He also gives us lollipops,
Just for being good.

I wish Mama would get a daytime
job,
Just like Danny's mom.
Danny seems so happy.

Robbie George

David said he saw Mama
On the corner of 14th and "V"
Last Saturday night;
He said she looked pretty, just like a
_____.

Then he and his friends laughed.
What do fifth-graders know
anyway.
I just stared at them;
Alex told them to leave me alone.

Mama,
We love you.
Please love us
And come home.

A VARIANT COLLECTION
PART II

ⱭꝂ

ABOVE THE CLOUDS

I flew above the clouds,
And caught the birth of a sunrise,
So tranquil, so majestic,
Exploding with shimmering golden rays,
Sprinkled over a sea of purity.

I floated above the clouds,
So peaceful, so calm,
Just like the lofty eagle,
 soaring on the wind;
All seemed at rest.

Mountains of white,
Shadows of black and gray,
Towering, tumbling, bumping,
Engendering streaks like fiery rhapsodies,
Bewildering the soul and mind.

Cast into a sea of mystery,
Oh! pillows of white,
Mountains like snow,
Tumbling, falling down below,

One can not fathom the essence of you;
I leave all to another's wit;
Your presence is so intense,
Your unleashed fury, so immense.

Like a mother's tender breast,
You bid me stay and rest;
Yet, some illusions foster deception;
Deception fosters finality.

DEED LEFT UNDONE

The immensity of my error,
The tragedy of an omission,
Has come to haunt each waking hour,
Searing my memory;

The mischance of a deed left undone,
Though wrought by innocence,
Comes menacing,
Like a heart torn asunder;

Time tarries for no one;
The moment has flown,
Opportunity has gone,
Broken hearts lie sinking in despair;

Yesterday seems so far away;
Clouded memories of things long ago,
Never to be touched once more,
And tomorrow is but an illusion.

The threads of life,
Are of a prevalent uncertainty,
inexplicably interwoven,
Into the fabric of existence;

Autumn sings a song of repose,
A melodious rhapsody of peace,
And a thrilling chill in the air,
Bodes a melody of farewell.

BIRTH

I tasted the sweetness of birth,
As I breathed the newness of life,
And inhaled a strange mixture of existence.

The essence of the deed,
Is evermore etched in time;
The memory is forever in your mind.

You became my link to a strange place;
I sought the sweet smell of your substance,
Often denied what was rightfully mine.

You were my lifeline;
You embraced me as I crossed over;
I cherish the divine essence of you.

Encircled by an invisible bond,
You bade me stay;
My journey had been arduous.

I struggled at your knee,
Adored, loved, though sometimes loathed;
I learned the markings early.

From the inception,
My instructions were there;
My will was there also.

A LONELY ROAD

My heart wanders afar;
My mind has taken flight;
I now walk a lonely road,
My shoulders bear a heavy load;

My steps are labored;
My eyes are dim;
My spring, summer, and fall, bade adieu;
The tremors echo through and through.

Life so willed this servant be,
Too late to taste the honey dew drops,
To run that distant mile,
To make having lived worthwhile.

Heart's too heavy to fathom
The wise man's thoughts;
My winter waxes old;
Only a lonely spirit stands bold.

THE TRANSFORMATION

In the throes of death, she slumps,
Yielding herself to nature's calling,
Just a moment in time;

For she in duty knows,
The moment is nigh,
For her timely repose.

She divinely yields,
All essence of herself,
To ensure life after her lamented demise.

She drops her seeds to the ground,
Often whisked away on an errant breeze,
To land on foreign soil.

The rain beats down, down, down,
Planting, nourishing, fulfilling,
Awakening life anew.

The sun hovers overhead,
Warming, rejuvenating,
All part of a bigger plan.

We watch, but never understand,
Not wise enough to comprehend,
Just how such a wonder unfolds.

Her beauty is sadly ephemeral;
Her seed's to rest for a time,
Then awaken and bloom in all its glory.

THE UNION

Sweet is love awakening;
Bitter is love's lonely demise.
Union without love is to
demoralize.

Like the early morning dew,
Encompassing all it touches,
Love penetrates the heart and soul
of you.

Like the fragrance of the fresh-
blown rose,
Intoxicating all it encompasses
Love, your essence will enclose.

Like the sun's eternal flame,
Kissing the earth with its tender
touch,
Love warms life's every frame.

After the promises have been made,
After the vows have been taken,
After the teary good-byes,
After the supreme consummation,

After the smiles and laughter,
After the miraculous creation,
After the tears and pains,
After love has been endlessly tested,

Will I relish your smile?
Will you seek my loving touch?
Will the bond remain unbroken?
Will our union have been
worthwhile?

I see your loving face;
I succumb to the fire in your eyes;
I feel your heart beating in rhythm
to mine;
I know our marriage is surely
divine.

HER LOVE

The power of love
Forms an unbreakable chain,
Like the rays of sunshine,
Linking earth to the cosmos.

It reaches and touches
The hearts and souls of creatures untold,
Echoing like a mother's love, ever so kind,
The whispering of a soul divine.

She moves on the wind, unseen, yet felt,
Penetrating the heart and mind of you;
Ravished by greed, day by day,
Caught in a web, like a spider's prey.

Weep no more for her,
She took flight, gone before the dawning light;
A lingering breeze, a ray of sunshine,
The fragrance of a cherished memory.

We knew we were special;
Her hugs and kisses told us so;
We knew we were special;
Her love shone in her eyes.

We knew we were special,
Her smile enraptured us;
Her spirit knows we are special;
She lives forever in our hearts.

COLORS

I come in many shades;
Some you see,
Others lie deep
Within my soul;

I am as black as midnight,
As white as the virgin snow,
I am muted shades,
That dwell in infinity.

One can never discern
Nor ever learn,
The shades
Of me.

The intensity is weak,
Like the wind on a still sunny morn;
It is strong,
Like the force, In a blue-black storm;

One can never fathom the essence of me;
My mood swings like a pendulum,
Forever in motion, like the tide,
And changing all bestride;

My essence is forever present,
Sculpturing, carving, coloring,
Endowing the spirit
Of me.

Robbie George

I cling, I toss and turn,
I crawl, I climb to discover,
To savor the newness of life,
To find the secrets of the rainbow.

I walk, I run,
I crawl, I struggle,
To find the meaning,
At the end.

THE SERVANT

I am a common person.
I mend hearts;
I mold minds;
I calm fears;

My days are long;
My nights are fraught
With unanswered questions;
My means are meager;

My rewards are priceless.
I love, I offer compassion,
I guide, I empower
You with wings of flight;

I motivate the weak
To seek heights of strength;
I inspire the desolate
To find comfort and hope.

I captivate the thirsty
And press them
To drink of knowledge;
I inspire them to boldness and creativity.

I challenge the strong
To seek and attain realms unknown,
To touch the heavens,
And explore the world of infinity.

Robbie George

I heal broken hearts;
I console the troubled, confused, bruised,
And mend contrite spirits;
I am a teacher.

I incite the bold
To touch an unknown realm,
To explore and dance with the stars,
To let their spirits soar.

I inspire all to seek and find
The beauty that lies
Within their souls,
The magnificent glory of their being.

I DON'T WANT TO LET YOU GO

I don't want to let you go,
But I must, I know;
I don't want to let you go,
But He has called you home.

I don't want to let you go,
I needed to say, "I love you,"
Ten thousand times and more;
But God's angels are swinging low.

I don't want to let you go;
You needed to pray with me,
Like you did many timers before;
I don't want to let you go.

Your laughter I needed to share,
But He said your stay has ended;
I don't want to let you go,
But He wants you so;

I needed to reminisce,
About the joys we used to share;
My heart aches when I remember
How we used to hug and kiss;

I don't want to let you go.
But the time has come to say good-bye.
The angels have swung low
To carry your soul home.

I sat and cried as your soul took flight;
I sat and cried as your body
Lay in heavenly array.
I don't want to let you go.

I sat and cried
As your face
Was hidden forever more;
I don't want to let you go.

I stood and cried as your body
Was lowered six feet below;
I stood and cried
As the earth upon your face was tossed.

I don't want to let you go;
My tears
Are but a catharsis
For my soul;

Why didn't I help,
When you asked for a guiding hand?
Why didn't I smile
As I nursed you day by day?

Why didn't I kneel in prayer,
When your burdens were too heavy to bear?
Why didn't I carry you,
When you fell along the way?

What deeds have I left undone?
Lord, forgive me, I pray;
Let me serve another day.
Let me guide a sinner from dismay..

The catacombs cry out;
The graves moan and voices shout;
The souls are restless;
What travesty have we wrought?

What pain have we left unattended,
What burdens have we not borne,
What crosses have we not shouldered,
What hearts have we scorned?

The heart and soul must lead.
What tasks have we left undone,
What joy have we not shared,
What race have we not run?

Could I have wrought a difference?
Could I have held you longer?
Many things I shall never know,
But my heart seeks peace, as I let you go.

I LOVE YOU

I love you,
In your most vulnerable moment,
When your guard is down,
Even when your brow wears a
frown.

I love you,
When you smile
With just a sparkle from your eyes,
When you breathe with sweet,
sweet sighs.

I love your peaceful serenity;
I love your captivating goodness,
When the sunlight warms your face,
Illuminating your womanly grace.

I love you ,
In your barest moment,
When your toes wiggle without a
sound,
And the pleasure echoes all around.

I love you,
When you touch me with your fire,
When you set my heart ablaze,
When I slump as in a daze.

I love your footsteps so light,
I love your touch so gentle,
I love the essence of your splendor
When our souls to each surrender.

I love the taste of you,
When together our hearts
Sing a melodious rhapsody,
Echoing my love for thee.

I love your needing me
And my needing you;
I love the sweet agony you cause
me,
And I cause you, when in an errant
fantasy.

I love you, because love is you;
I love the ecstasy we share,
When we entwine,
One in body, heart, soul and mind.

'TIS REALITY

ॐ

MAKE IT LEGIT

You're bumming around, your spirit's
down,
You don't know which way to go;
Just ask for help from above,
He will never say, "No";
Look to the One who is infinite;
He can show you how to make life legit.

So, you've been mistreated, abused,
You need somebody to love you;
Heck, you've got to first love yourself,
And learn to love others too;
You sound like a first-class hypocrite;
You have to work to make life legit.

You don't like yourself?
Well, it's a dirty shame;
You are so special;
You were created in His name;
Your offspring will surely benefit,
If you make your living legit.

So, you're gonna let life play you cheap,
And allow misery to ride your hide;
Get yourself together,
Look for that angel to stand by your side;
Stop acting like a nitwit;
Strive to make your life legit.

Robbie George

Nobody ever said you're great?
Well, your mind is like a fine machine,
Yearning, waiting to be tuned;
You have talents others have never seen;
Your heart and mind you must commit;
It takes you to make your life legit.

Look in life's mirror,
Examine what you see;
You have it; it's you;
That's who you will always be;
When the world thinks you're a misfit,
Build your dreams, show your life is legit;

Just accept you as you are;
It's deep down inside,
Where you will find,
That beauty and love reside;
From your talents all can benefit;
Use them to reveal your life is legit.

You say you have no dad;
You've got no hope,
Mama's no good,
So you've turned to dope;
Weeds and powder have no benefit;
Using and dealing drugs is not legit.

You're dancing with death;
You can become the living dead,
With no heart, no soul,
Brain dead in your head;
You're exposed to diseases others transmit;
That's no way to make living legit.

Man, that's stupid, stupid, stupid;
You say you can't cope,
Bogey-man's beating you down;
Don't know how to climb life's rope;
Life's hard, but you can't quit,
To survive, you must make life legit;

TWO

You've got to use your head;
Learn how the equation works;
Then you will discover that
Stupidity is only for lazy jerks;
Build your skyscrapers with your wit;
Prove life can be wonderful and legit.

Stay in school while you can;
Education is a powerful key;
It can help get that job you need,
And divorce you from poverty;
In your heart and mind you must commit,
To make your life legit.

Pick your teachers' minds;
They've walked the walk;
They have the experience you need;
They can talk the talk;
While traveling life's rocky road, don't quit,
You're learning how to make life legit;

Teachers have traveled life's alleys,
They know the back roads,
And the bright highways;
They carry the heaviest loads;
Their experiences, you must admit,
Can show you how to make life legit.

There's a great way to start your day;
Go to the library, read a book;
There's gold in that place,
You just have to take time and look;
Don't make ignorance your bottomless pit,
Learn to make your life legit.

THREE

Social Services are never enough?
Your life's a living hell?
You don't know what to do?
So, you hate, get mad and rebel;
Since you're blessed with mother-wit,
Use it to make your life legit.

You need food, shelter, love and respect;
Use your hands, feel your sweat;
Make your family more secure;
Honest labor you won't regret;
It's OK to toil and "bust the grit;"
It's smart to make your actions legit.

You want to have babies to feel grown-up;
All animals know how to breed;
Can you teach, discipline, and protect?
Can you shelter, clothe, and feed?
Don't make your child a misfit;
Good parents make parenting legit.

FOUR

You talk about respect;
Respect yourself, friends, and mama too.
Check out your nasty attitude;
Positive actions you must pursue;
Stop being a hypocrite,
It's time you made your act legit.

Invest in your future: learn a trade;
Work a sixteen-hour day;
Feel your power and strength;
Be wise and save your pay;
Your future can become more definite,
When you strive to make your life legit.

Robbie George

Life's hard at every turn?
Well, this is a wake-up call;
Fervently build your skyscrapers,
Or through the cracks you will surely fall;
Into life's scheme, you can become a fit,
Just strive to make your life legit.

You can feel and think; you are unique;
So Mr. Public Opinion sounds pretty bad,
Get to know your assets and liabilities,
Or your future can be painfully sad;
Don't disintegrate while you sit;
Do your part to make your life legit.

You've never held a job?
It's an honor to get dirt on your hand;
Sweat and toil help make the man;
So, step up and take a stand;
Positive attitude is a prerequisite,
To help make your life legit.

FIVE

You say you're in a gang;
You're seeking power and fame;
Body's changing, hormones raging,
Can't take the group down in shame;
You've been ordered to make a hit;
That's no way to make life legit.

The system has you confused;
You're trapped by dishonesty and greed;
You can't take anything with you;
So earn and use what you need.
Be wise and admit,
Living's better when you're legit.

Cheating and lying can't be your gain;
They stain your heart and soul,
And destroy life's harmony;
Commit your mind to self-control;
Life's too precious to wallow in a dark pit;
You can feel the sunshine when legit.

Killing and stealing is so insane;
There's no good in either crime;
They only bring heartache and pain,
And will take you down in your prime;
Crossing over the line is the pit;
Control yourself, be legit.

The cattle pen's no place to be;
There's no freedom, no air, no sunshine,
No moon, no stars at night;
Your body and soul it will confine;
Your stay could be infinite;
It's wise to make your life legit.

There's danger behind those bars;
There're snakes looking for a prey like you;
To them, you're only meat;
Death lurks through and through;
No living soul can ever fit;
You've got to make your life legit;

SIX

You can't change yesterday,
But you can help shape tomorrow;
Your future can bring happiness,
So stop wallowing in pity and sorrow.
Life's what you'll permit;
It takes soul to make living legit.

You are an original masterpiece;
There is no one like you;
Get to know who you are;
Discover your treasures, and when you do,
You will know you're not a misfit;
Life is good when it's legit.

Know what is expected of you;
Society has got to have some rules;
Be aware of what they are;
Those who abuse them are stupid fools.
Don't let life become counterfeit;
Use the rules to make it legit.

Now, don't procrastinate;
Reach for higher ground,
Start your journey today,
Don't let your lazy body just hang around;
The effort is for your benefit;
There's no reason not to be legit.

Build upon your dreams;
Make them great and tall;
Reality is an awesome high;
Just don't try to walk before you crawl;
Utilize your mother-wit;
It's a tool to help make life legit.

You are clever and smart;
Create your successes, big and small,
Be proud of what you do;
You can build your own "Taj Mahal;"
From your talents you will benefit,
When you make them legit.

SEVEN

Look at the sky;
Feel the breeze in your face;
Watch the birds as they fly by;
There's amazing power in this place;
Let your heart and soul admit,
Your living can become legit.

Whenever you are sad and down,
And you don't know what to do,
Remember you are His child;
He promised to rescue and comfort you;
To Him your troubles submit,
Through faith, He will make your life legit.

OF HUMANESS

I was seduced on yesterday;
I am a queen, mere man is he;
And though you say 'tis unbelieving,'
A more fulfilling love can nev'r be.

No time can ever be claimed;
I stood at his brier and thought as I wept,
The loss is mine to be borne,
You will not his memory have kept.

Friends, of humanness pretended to be;
When grief so enclosed, my soul I exposed;
You slashed and lashed at my wounds,
Ere my heart became composed;

But, he who in agony suffers,
Tender wisdom is his due;
More meaningful humanness becomes;
Now, I can truly love and console you.

Robbie George

SHADES OF SADNESS

Time waits for no one;
Like the wind on its unseen way,
Changing the essence of being,
It silently moves without delay,
Sometimes leaving painful questions.

Her Grandma died
When she was very young;
Wasted time, unsolved mysteries;
She didn't love the grandchild,
Whose skin was a different hue.

She never got the chance
To feel the love of her own,
Who truly loved her,
And longed to be held
In her strong, warm arms.

Time bore an age of innocence;
It offered a calming influence;
Bombarded with the newness of life,
Ignorant of the passing,
Just aware the journey had begun.

While growing up in open spaces,
This child's hours were filled,
Playing and imagining;
She never had to wait for the next day,
For her, it simply came.

She never intended to dream,
While the days slipped away,
Unaware of life,
And the many challenges it offered,
Or the responsibilities it demanded.

Youth came crashing into her sphere,
Mysterious, consuming,
Yet full of promise;
Robust, carefree, rising to the call
Of natural challenges.

She wanted to believe the change was gradual,
But she did not watch as it came,
Nor did she feel at ease
With the strange, new awakening;
Newness requires assimilation.

Her troubled grandma left too soon,
Not yet knowing
When she met her,
She did not recognize
Who she was.

MEMPHIS

It sits on the banks of the
Mississippi,
Once a brilliant jewel of the Mid-
South;
Fire on the mountain top,
Flames in the valley so low,
Bereft of her glory and opulence.

Through and through lies a
lamentable plight;
Where there was once pride,
It now wallows in degradation;
Where there was once integrity,
It stumbles in gripping avarice.

A surface, superficial,
All too soon fades away;
Where there was once
enlightenment,
Stands woeful ignorance and decay;
Fear and distrust permeate.

Invaded by a deadly plague,
That gnaws at its heart, soul and
sinew;
Hate knows no boundaries;
Silently, viciously, it spreads its
tentacles,

Like acid rain in a blinding storm.

When the heart becomes drunk with
vanity,
And hard like stone,
When the noblesse oblige system
becomes faulty,
And deceitfulness disdains the
desolate,
Pain and suffering abound.

A stigma laces it through and
through;
Like a virulent undertow,
It claims its victims ere they know,
You can't press a raging tiger to
your breast;
Maim it must; devour it can.

When seething cauldrons of enmity,
Spread turmoil, shame and deceit,
When apathy and greed,
Secretly simmer in a chaotic
infirmary,
Deadly forces control and corrupt.

When the heart embraces aloofness
As a viable solution to normalcy,
When a hungry child wanders
without hope,

When morality becomes but a
tattered discourse,
Streams of despair ripple like an
aftershock.

When love loses its savor,
And becomes a blinding antipathy,
When the will is weak,
And the heart and soul are
decadent,
Destruction comes from within.

When juvenile minds dwell in old
heads,
Who taint, distort and destroy,
When a city ignores its walking
dead,
And tolerates the underlying
causation,
Lost are tomorrow's dreams, hopes
and freedom.

When the soul of the city,
Become bereft, debauch and
decadent,
When the heart becomes hollow and
unfeeling,
And men run with no escape in
flight,
Extinction looms on the horizon.

Must one say, "It sat high above the
Mississippi,
Where it became one with thee;
Were they wise, they could but tell,
Just how a great city fell?"
Hope does dwell deep in the souls
of men.

ŋ

ACKNOWLEDGMENTS

Some of the material in this book evolved over the span of four decades. Some of the material was started less than four years ago. Over the years I have intensively observed human strength and human frailty. I have observed human problems that seem insurmountable. In searching for answers and solutions, I discovered that many problems are vast, dark, and heavy. I have been inspired to address some of those problems. I hope what I have written will inspire others to open their eyes, hearts, and minds and be compelled to help effect a solution.

My close-knit family has always been an integral part of my life. My three brothers and I grew up in country parsonages. The experiences were most rewarding. We did not know we were poor because we had love, direction, food, and shelter. I truly thank my parents. I thank my husband, children and grandchildren, who are an inspiration to me. I thank my sons and daughters-in-law for my grandchildren. I thank my daughter, Carolyn, for mirroring my image, and my niece, Tannera, for her technical assistance.

I thank my friends, Bettye Radden, Janet Bucklaw, Tricia Goolsby and Gloria Cox for their critical analyses. I thank my friend, Dorothy Hibler, for inspiring me to view life from a much deeper perception. Most of all, I thank God for inspiration. I thank Him too, for directing my footsteps.

About the Author

I grew up with three brothers, in country parsonages, in several small Mississippi towns.

I learned that poverty comes in many diverse forms. As children, we did not possess material wealth, but, we had the wealth of two loving, caring parents. We felt content and secure, knowing they would provide food, clothes, and shelter. They also provided positive directions and lots of love.

We were taught to appreciate life, to work hard, to be respectable, and to love each other. These lessons and experiences were invaluable. They served as a model to me as a person, and subsequently, a mother.

I have also seen the concomitant effects on my children and their children.

I am a retired schoolteacher. I taught elementary education for twenty-six years in Washington, D. C. As a teacher, I tried to share, with my students, some of the lessons I learned as a child.

I relocated from Maryland to Memphis, Tennessee, in 1998, and although I have found it difficult to adjust to the city, I have written several of my more serious poems in this societal climate. I find that much inspiration comes from my experiences here.

Many of the children of this century are not being afforded the bare necessities of life – food, clothes, shelter, sensible directions, and love.

I truly believe, "Things that grow need positive directions, thoughtful attention, and unconditional love to flourish."

Printed in the United States
19429LVS00001B/100-291